A Kid's Guide to

Origami™

Making ORIGAMI PAPER AIRPLANES Step by Step

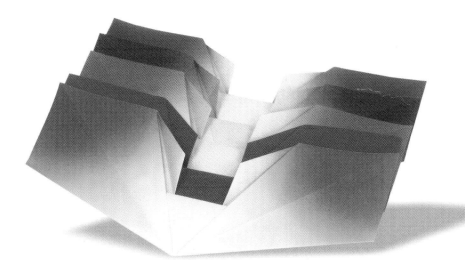

Michael G. LaFosse

The Rosen Publishing Group's

PowerKids Press™

New York

To Uncle Norman LaFosse, who patiently taught me how to fold my first paper airplanes

Published in 2004 by The Rosen Publishing Group, Inc.
29 East 21st Street, New York, NY 10010

First Edition

Editors: Jannell Khu
Book Design: Emily Muschinske
Layout Design: Kim Sonsky

Illustration Credits: Michael G. LaFosse
Photographs by Cindy Reiman, background image of paper crane on each page © CORBIS.

LaFosse, Michael G.
Making origami paper airplanes step by step / Michael G. LaFosse.
     v. cm. — (A kid's guide to origami)
Includes bibliographical references and index.
Contents: What is origami? — Safe-t dart — Two-piece stunt plane — Two-piece jet — Stacking wings — Squid plane — Huck Finn — Stunt double — Art-Deco wing.
ISBN 0-8239-6700-X
1. Paper airplanes—Juvenile literature. 2. Origami—Juvenile literature. [1. Paper airplanes. 2. Origami. 3. Handicraft.] I. Title. II. Series.
TL778 .L34 2004
736'.982—dc21
                                    2002151416

Manufactured in the United States of America

Contents

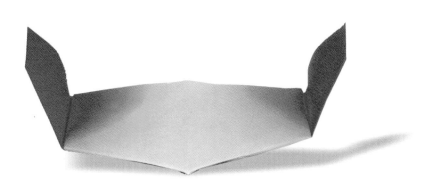

What Is Origami?

People throughout the world enjoy origami. Origami is the art of folding paper to make different shapes. Origami is a Japanese word. *Ori* means "fold" and *kami* means "paper." Thousands of toys, animals, and boxes can be created by folding paper. New designs are invented every day by beginners and **experts** alike.

Paper is easy to find, and you won't need special tools for origami. Just be sure that the paper you use is the right shape and size for the origami project. Origami directions are shown with special **symbols**. You will need to know a few origami symbols to make origami shapes. These symbols are explained at the back of the book on page 22.

Once you learn origami symbols, you can understand an origami book from any country, even from Japan! This origami book is about one of my favorite subjects, folding paper airplanes. Origami paper planes are fun to fold and fun to fly. After you learn the basics of folding origami airplanes, you will enjoy experimenting with different airplane shapes and using different kinds of paper. Some of the airplanes in this book use square paper. Origami paper, which is already cut into squares, is thin, easy to fold, and is a good choice. If you are using origami paper to make any origami shape, make sure you start with the white side facing up. You can also cut paper squares from any kind of paper. Try using paper of different sizes and thicknesses. The most important thing is to be creative and have fun!

Safe-T Dart

Leonardo da Vinci (1452–1519) was a famous Italian artist and inventor. Many people believe he created the first paper airplane. Da Vinci's work still **inspires** people today. For instance, most people have folded a paper dart airplane by the time they enter grade school. This is one of da Vinci's **designs**. You can invent, too! You can fold the wings to make a different shape, or you can add folded fins. This origami airplane is a **variation** of da Vinci's paper airplane. Unlike da Vinci's paper airplane, this model does not have a sharp point, which can hurt someone's eye. That is why this airplane is called the Safe-T Dart.

1

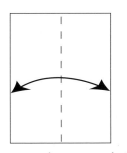

Start with an 8 ½-by-11-inch (21.6-x-27.9-cm) paper. Valley fold the paper in half lengthwise. Unfold. You made a center crease line.

2

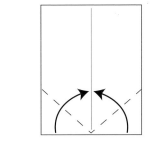

Valley fold the bottom corners to the center crease line. The bottom part of the plane should look like a triangle as shown below in step 3.

3

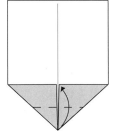

Valley fold the sharp triangle point to the two center corners. This fold is what makes the plane a Safe-T Dart.

4

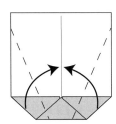

Study the slanted dotted lines before you fold. After you're done with this step, the two folded corners should meet at the center crease line.

5

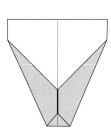

Your plane should look like the above. The next step is to fold the plane lengthwise along the center crease. The folds of the paper should be outside.

6

Turn the plane so that the Safe-T Dart's nose is facing left. Make sure the open part of the plane is facing upward. Valley fold the side that's facing you, and mountain fold the other side.

7

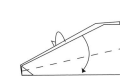

Back view of wings

Open the two wings. Your Safe-T Dart should look like the above drawing from the back view. Now see how far your plane can fly!

Two-Piece Stunt Plane

Origami designs made from two or more papers are called **compound** models. This origami airplane gets its name because it is made with two pieces of paper. It is called a **stunt** plane because it can fly through the air and do fancy loops and curvy dips. Do flying **experiments** with your stunt airplane. Curl up the two back corners of the wings to make your stunt airplane loop. Does it fly differently if you curl the corners just a little, or a lot, or if you curl them down instead of up? How does the plane fly when you throw it fast, or slow, or if you just let it drop? Have fun finding out!

1

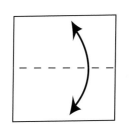

Use two 8-½-inch-(21.6-cm) square papers. Use two different colors of paper to make your plane look especially nice. Valley fold and unfold the first paper. You've made a center crease. This will be the rear, main wing section.

2

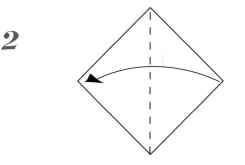

Position the other paper so that it looks like a diamond shape. Use the dotted lines as a guide to fold from the right to the left corner. Now you have a triangle. This will be the front wing section.

3

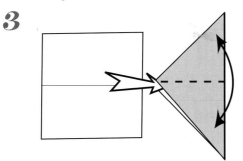

Fold and unfold the triangle to make a center crease. Slip the rear, main wing section completely inside the front wing section. Be sure to line up the center creases on both pieces of paper.

4

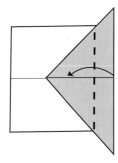

Look at the dotted line before you fold. Next carefully fold the wide end of the triangle along the dotted line.

5

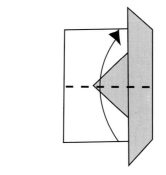

Valley fold the plane. Make sure you fold along the center crease line as shown by the dotted line.

6

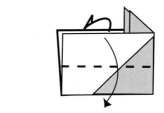

Valley fold the side that's facing you, and mountain fold the other side. Make sure you fold so that the upper straight edge of the wings meets at the bottom edges of the plane. Open the wings straight out. You are now ready to fly your plane! Try folding up the back part of the plane wings to see it do neat loops!

Two-Piece Jet

All the paper airplanes in this book are **gliders**. They do not have **propulsion**, which means that they do not have engines or motors. The first motorized flying machines used **propellers** to help them travel through the air. Later, the jet engine was invented. This allowed planes to travel at greater speeds. Faster planes use smaller wings, and the shape of a plane's **fuselage** allows it to fly through the air like a bullet or an arrow. This paper airplane is called a jet because of its shape. It is designed to fly straight, far, and fast. This plane is a good design to make if you want to have target **competitions** with your friends.

1

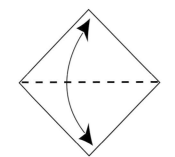

Use an 8-inch (20.3-cm) square paper. Position one of the papers so that it is diamond shaped. Valley fold and unfold. You have made a crease line.

2

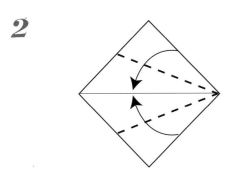

Valley fold the top corner to the center crease line. Valley fold the bottom corner to the center line. Notice that these folds are angled.

3

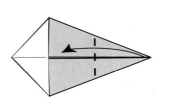

Fold the narrow end to the bottom edge of the triangle you created in the last step. Use the dotted line as a guide.

4

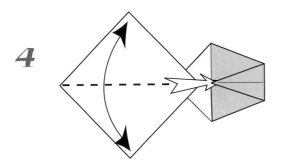

Valley fold the second paper and unfold. Slip the right corner of this paper inside the first paper. Be sure to line up the creases.

5

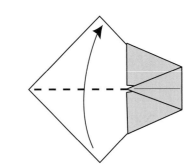

Valley fold in half along the center crease.

6

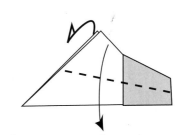

Valley fold the wing facing you, and mountain fold the other side. The front top edge should line up with the bottom fold.

7

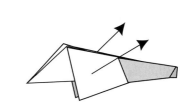

Open the wings and throw the plane!

8

Back view of wings

This is how the back view of the wings should look.

11

Stacking Wings

This origami project will show you why some paper planes fly farther than others. It has to do with the plane's shape and **resistance**. Take two sheets of paper the same size. Throw one into the air. Crumple the other sheet into a ball and throw it. The crumpled paper travels farther because it is **denser** and has less air resistance. Fold a Stacking Wing and you will see that the tail has only one paper layer, but the front has many layers. The front is denser than the tail. This means that the front will have less resistance in the air than the tail. Fly one Stacking Wing and see how it flies. Next stack several Stacking Wings one inside another and see how far they fly!

1

Use an 8-inch (20.3-cm) square paper. Position the paper so that it looks like a diamond shape. Valley fold. You will have a triangle shape as shown in the next step.

2

Carefully take the left and right ends of the triangle and valley fold so that they meet up at the center corner. Unfold.

3

Look at the dotted line above for guidance. Valley fold the first layer of the top corner. The drawing below shows how it will look after you do this fold. Good job!

4

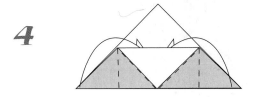

Carefully valley fold, and slip the two side corners behind the center folded corner. If you've done this correctly, you will have made a pocket! Look at step 5 to see how the shape should look after you've done this step.

5

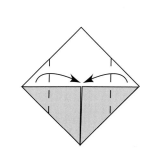

Fold the left and right side corners so that they meet at the center.

6

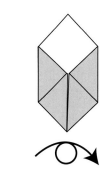

Turn the Stacking Wing over.

7

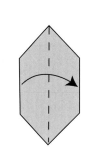

Fold in half lengthwise, edge to edge. Fold so that all your folds are on the outside.

8

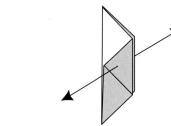

Open the Stacking Wing and flatten. Throw the wing into the air and watch it fly high over your head.

Squid Plane

After you fold this paper plane, you will see why it is called the Squid Plane. The plane resembles the body of a squid! In many countries, printer paper is a little longer and narrower than the printer paper used in the United States. The paper's **proportions** make it a true rectangle. The true rectangle shape is ideal for making the Squid Plane. The printer paper used in the United States measures 8 ½ by 11 inches (21.6 x 27.9 cm). The size is too big to make a perfect Squid Plane. The **canard wings** of a Squid Plane are too wide when folded from this paper. This makes the plane **stall**. However, you can correct this by adding two folds to the canard wings.

1

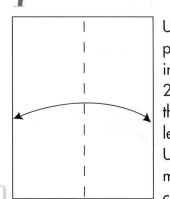

Use a printer paper 8 ½ by 11 inches (21.6 x 27.9 cm). Fold the paper in half lengthwise. Unfold. You have made a center crease.

2

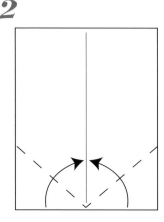

Carefully valley fold each of the bottom corners to meet at the center crease line. The Safe-T Dart on page 7 uses this fold in step 2.

3

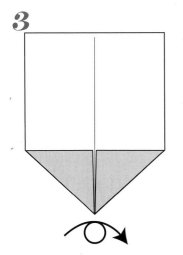

Turn the paper over so the folds are facing down. The pointed part is the nose of the Squid Plane.

4

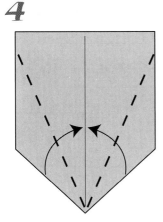

Valley fold the two edges on either side so that they meet at the center crease line. Look at the next step to see how it should appear.

5

Pull out the two corners from behind the nose. Look at step 6 to see how the shape should appear. Notice that the front of the plane looks diamond shaped.

6

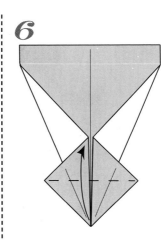

Valley fold the diamond shape. You've made the canard wings. Do you see the two triangles, one inside the other? Look at step 7 for help.

7

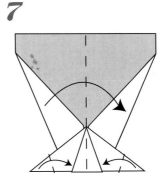

Valley fold the two corner points of the canard wing. Use the dotted lines to help you make this fold. Next fold the paper in half, wing to wing, so that the folds are inside.

8

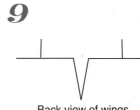

Valley fold the side facing you and mountain fold the other side. Make sure to match the flat wing edges to the bottom edge of the plane.

9

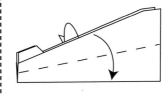

Back view of wings

Open the wings and lift up the two tips of the canard wing. This is how your Squid Plane should appear from the back.

Huck Finn

Mark Twain (1835–1910) is a famous American author. One of his best-known characters is Huckleberry Finn, from the book *The Adventures of Huckleberry Finn*. Huck was **mischievous**. When Huck got into trouble, his luck got him out of trouble! This plane is called the Huck Finn because it has the same spirit and luck as Huck! You can throw it into the air any which way and it will recover and land nicely and safely. The open space under the paper plane's nose can be used for special **launches**. Put your pointing finger inside this space and whip your arm forward to send it quickly into the air. The faster the flight, the more the plane will loop!

1

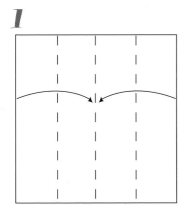

Use 8-inch- (20.3-cm-) square paper. Fold in half lengthwise. Unfold. Fold the outer edges to the center crease. Do not unfold.

2

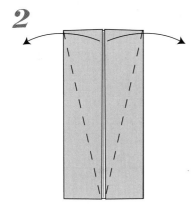

Use the dotted lines to help you fold in this step. Valley fold the two top inside corners outward. Look at step 3 to see how it will appear after you fold.

3

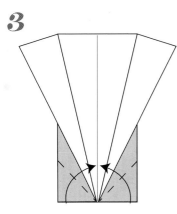

Valley fold the bottom corners to meet at the center crease line. Look at step 4 to see how it should appear. Do you see a triangle shape?

Valley fold the triangle shape to the base. Valley fold again to the place where the tip of the triangle touches the center line. You will see a rectangle shape.

4

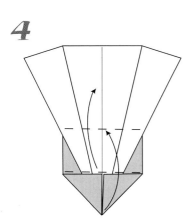

5

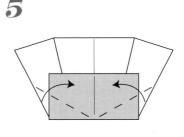

Valley fold the bottom two corners to make a point. Notice that their edges do not meet at the center crease line.

6

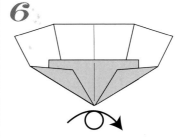

Turn the Huck Finn over so that all the folds face downward.

7

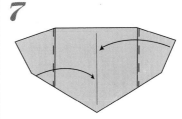

Valley fold the wings. Next, open up the two wings. Now your Huck Finn is ready for some flying adventures!

Double-Flap Plane

Real airplanes have flaps on their wings to make the planes move in different directions. Flaps called elevators make the plane climb or **descend**. An aileron is a flap that makes the plane **bank** for a turn. Some planes have a **vertical** flap called a rudder on the tail. The rudder also helps the plane turn. This paper plane has elevons on its main wings. An elevon flap combines the **function** of an elevator and aileron. The folds for the elevons are in step 5. As an experiment, fold one plane with elevons and one without. You will see the importance of the flaps.

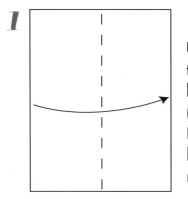

Use printer paper that measures 8 ½ by 11 inches (21.6 x 27.9 cm). Fold it in half lengthwise, left to right.

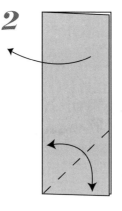

Valley fold the bottom corner. Take care to match it to the long, open edge on the right. Unfold and open the paper completely.

3

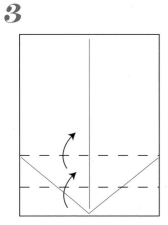

Do you see a triangle shape? Valley fold twice, one at a time, along the dotted lines. The folds need to be the same size. Make the first fold so that it meets the top of the wide end of the triangle shape, as shown by the dotted lines.

4

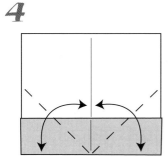

Valley fold the left and the right corners of the bottom folded edge to meet at the center crease. Unfold.

5

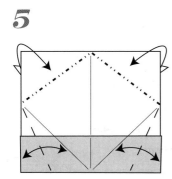

Mountain fold the two upper corners back. Unfold. Valley fold the bottom corners up to meet the crease lines that you made in step 4. Unfold. Good work!

6

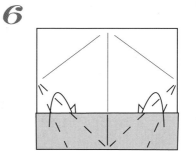

Tuck the bottom corners behind the folded edge of paper. Use the creases made in steps 4 and 5.

7

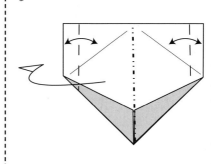

Valley fold the side edges to form the fins. Unfold. Mountain fold the plane in half, wing to wing, so that the folded V-shaped layers remain on the outside.

8

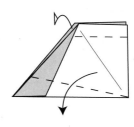

Position the plane so that the nose faces left. Valley fold the wing twice on the side that's facing you, as shown. Mountain fold the wing twice on the other side.

Art-Deco Wing

Art deco is an art style that was popular in the 1920s and the 1930s. Clean lines and simple shapes are

some characteristics of art deco. I've named this paper model the Art-Deco Wing because the design is simple and modern. This wing has a very low angle of **descent** in flight. This means that it will glide almost level with the ground and stay in the air much longer than a plane with a higher angle of descent. This plane is a good stunt plane, too. Throw it with extra force to make it do loops!

1

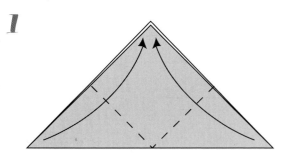

Use 8 ½-inch- (21.6-cm-) square paper. Valley fold to make a triangle shape. Valley fold the two side corners up to the top corner.

2

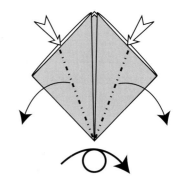

One at a time, open each of the two corners to form a cone shape. Next flatten each cone shape so that it looks like a kite shape. Turn the plane over. Look at step 3 to see how it should appear.

3

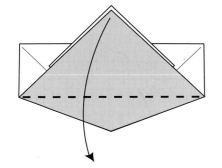

Valley fold the top corner to the dotted line. Look at step 4 to see how your plane should appear.

4

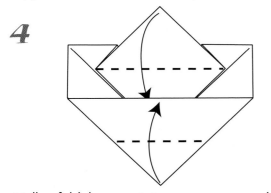

Valley fold the remaining top corner and slip it inside the pocket you made in step 3. Valley fold the bottom corner so that the point meets the top fold.

5

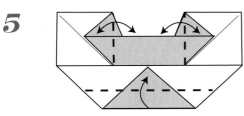

Valley fold the bottom at the dotted line. Fold each corner at the dotted line. Unfold.

6

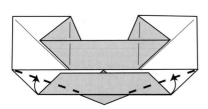

Valley fold the two bottom corners so that the edges meet the horizontal, folded edge.

7

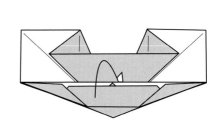

Mountain fold and slip the front layer in the center into the pocket you made in step 3.

8

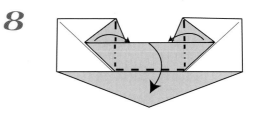

Fold down the folded edge. The left and right corners will move toward each other. Flatten the paper by pushing the folded edges closest to you so they line up with the edge.

9

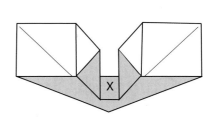

Tuck the X tab into the nose pocket you made in step 3.

10

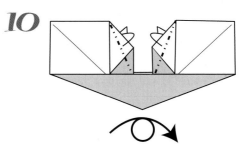

Mountain fold each of the two corner layers around to the other side of the paper. Turn the wing over and let it fly!

Origami Key

1. MOUNTAIN FOLD

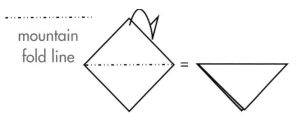

mountain fold line

Notice the mountain fold line. To make a mountain fold, fold the paper back away from you, so that it meets at the other side.

2. VALLEY FOLD

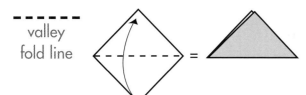

valley fold line

Notice the valley fold line. To make a valley fold, fold the paper towards you.

3. MOVE, PULL, PUSH, SLIP

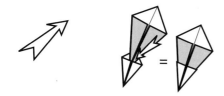

4. DIRECTION ARROW

5. FOLD and UNFOLD

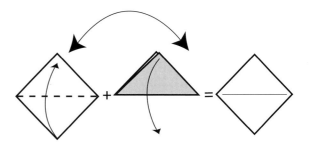

6. TURNOVER

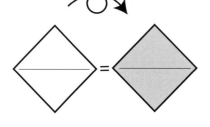

7. ROTATE

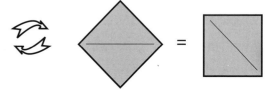

8. CUT

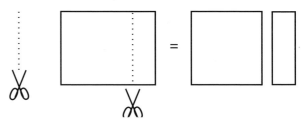

9. REPEAT

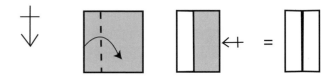

Glossary

bank (BANK) To turn, in flight, by lowering one wing.

canard wings (kuh-NARD WINGZ) Wings mounted on the front end of an airplane.

competitions (kom-pih-TIH-shinz) Games or tests.

compound (KOM-pownd) Two or more things combined.

denser (DENTS-er) More closely packed together or thicker.

descend (dih-SEND) To travel downward.

descent (dih-SENT) Downward motion.

designs (dih-ZYNZ) Plans or the form of something.

experiments (ex-SPER-uh-ments) Tests done on things to learn more about them.

experts (EK-sperts) People who know a lot about a subject.

function (FUNK-shun) Use or purpose.

fuselage (FYOO-suh-loj) An aircraft's body, not including the wings or the tail.

gliders (GLY-derz) Aircraft that fly without a motor.

inspires (in-SPYRZ) Fills with excitement about something.

launches (LONCH-ez) Pushes out or puts into the air.

mischievous (MIS-chuh-vis) To be playful and sometimes get into trouble.

propellers (pruh-PEL-erz) Paddlelike parts on an object that spin to move the object forward.

proportions (pruh-POR-shunz) The measure of one part compared to another.

propulsion (pruh-PUL-shun) The force that moves something.

resistance (rih-ZIS-tens) A strong stand taken against something.

stall (STOL) To come to a stop.

stunt (STUNT) An act that needs special skills or strength to do.

symbols (SIM-bulz) Objects or designs that stand for something else.

variation (ver-ee-AY-shun) A different way of doing something.

vertical (VER-tih-kul) In an up-and-down direction.

Index

Web Sites

Due to the changing nature of Internet links, PowerKids Press has developed an online list of Web sites related to the subject of this book. This site is updated regularly. Please use this link to access the list:
www.powerkidslinks.com/kgo/airplane/